Love a good fish story? Here are a few and they are true!

CLAY POND & OTHER FISH TAILS

Don G. Ford

ALL RIGHTS RESERVED

Dedication:

This book is dedicated to readers of good non-fiction storytelling. Sometimes stories that are true can sound so unreal. Maybe the word Creative would fit better here.

Creative Non-Fiction Storytelling - told in a way that sounds unbelievable, but still it really happened.

LEGEND OF CLAY POND

by Don Ford

It looked as if it were going to storm and get nasty, and I was without my rain gear. My heart leapt out of my throat, as I watched him flop on the surface of the water. He was on my line! Somehow he had taken the bait.

Not twenty minutes ago, my brother had the same fish on his line. He too was excited to see that massive fish making such a splash in Clay Pond. We all had heard stories, but lost our breath as the legend loomed before us. The monster of the deep, that others could only tell about, had never been caught by anyone, and was within our grasp.

For the next several minutes, he struggled to get free of my line, but I had him by his bootstraps. He was mine and that's all there was to it. The three of us could practically taste our prize. My neighbor, Phil, had hooked it the first time, and then it wiggled free of his line.

My brother told the same story, as it gobbled up his worm. He thought for sure he was going to nail it and pull it in. But our smart fish got his line all tangled in the duckweeds, and he managed to free himself from that second encounter.

I recall the words of my uncle, who has since passed on. "Give the fish some room to bite. Wait until he is done playing with his food and your line starts to move straight away from you. Now, right now, is when you pull quickly and set the hook. He's yours for sure."

Uncle Red was a trophy hunter and fisherman, and though he has gone on to fish in that eternal pool in the sky, his words will continue living in my memory. I also recall a time when he took me on my first hunting trip for quail. After I was spooked by the flurry of feathers and the whooshing sound they made at take off, I managed to blow several nice round holes in the sky. One bird was not ten feet from me, and I fired right at him, but he just slowly walked away. I swore I heard him laughing.

I became known as Deadeye after those little episodes. So fishing is my game. And I usually get my man every time. This day would be no exception. The legend of the pond was securely within my reach. Hundreds had tried before me, but no one could bring him in. This would be my finest hour.

Was he as big as everyone had told us? Yes he was, all that and more. His big black eyes just looked right through me. I could hardly believe what was right in front of me. The folklore told about this bullhead had ended. No more legendary fish in Clay Pond, just a trophy for my wall.

After putting up quite a show of force, my captured friend was secure in our bucket, hanging half out, while flipping madly about. He didn't come close to fitting in this five-gallon container. That's how big he was. How were we going to get him home? This I asked myself. He would probably flop out on the way there.

My brother then piped up. "Don, what are you going to do with her?" I was surprised at his comment.

"Her, what her?" He was right; this was a female and a mother about to spawn. Her stomach protruded greatly. Her young were alive and swimming inside her. We couldn't possibly remove her from Clay Pond. She was about to have her babies, and we would feel guilty if they all died.

Our neighbor said what we were all thinking. "She has to go back in the water." We all agreed, and the next thing I saw, as my heart returned to its place in my chest, was the great fish going below the surface of the water. It never returned to even say thank you. The legend was still intact. Besides, who knows but what the little ones would some day grow to become legends of the pond too.

Author Notes

When a bullhead is on your line, you will know it. They put up as good a fight as any fish possibly could. It is such a rush to finally secure the fish that others could only talk about, but you have it to show.

My Uncle Red took me fishing once to a stream near where we lived in Western, N.Y. We both fished this mile stretch of water to only yield one small brook trout. My uncle then opened up the fish to reveal what it was eating, and it wasn't worms. It was crayfish spawning time and little pink babies were in the fish's stomach.

We then went down to the shallows and lifted up rocks to find the crayfish, removed their young, and fished the same mile stretch again; this time using the new bait. We caught 22 more fish between us. I will always be indebted to my uncle for teaching me little secrets of fishing. I love my time spent along the streams and waterways, and for good reason. Thanks Uncle Red!

A Fish Story

by Don Ford

First Published in 2006 in Adirondack Life Magazine (This is a true story that happened to this author)

There was the time that my brother and I caught a giant frog and let it go. No one believed us. On another occasion we opened a freshwater clam and found a black pearl. This time everyone believed us, as we showed it around. But the strangest story of them all took place during my days as a forestry student at Paul Smith's college in 1968.

If you quizzed me on how many times during my 50-plus years I found myself back in the Adirondack Mountains, I'd come up with a high number and still miss a time or two.

It could be the lure of the lakes, rivers, and streams that bring me back. Maybe its adventures like the one at Cold River, when another student and I slept in a lean-to on the bank. At about five a.m. a whip- poor-will, calling out its name, awakened us. We came to fish, to sleep, and to dream. A short time later we made a trip to Ausable Chasm. I invited along a friend from the college, and he invited two students from Thailand. When we reached the water, we began to fish. Our classmates from Thailand did not have any gear, so we were going to share our poles and bait with them. They had other plans.

They rolled up their pants and waded into the Ausable River. Placing both hands in the water, they began to clap. To our surprise they both brought up fish in their bare hands. My roommate and I looked at each other and thought, 'why should they have all the luck?' We threw down our poles and into the water we went, clapping all the way. Before long we clapped up a few of our own fish. We brought our catch back to the dorm and enjoyed it with egg-drop soup, prepared by our Thai classmates.

This story gets stranger. A few years later I was at home recounting my fish tale to a grandmother and her eight-year-old grandson. The boy was really enjoying this one, and near the end of the story he left the house. About 15 minutes later he returned. In his absence the grandmother had listened to the end of the tale and doubled over laughing. The grandson waited for her to compose herself before holding up his trophy, a sucker.

He explained that he had gone down to the stream behind our house and clapped in the water. The fish swam into his hands and he lifted it out of the water in total amazement. The red-faced grandmother gathered up her grandson and left the house in silence. But don't throw away your tackle. I still fish with a pole. What chance would the fish have if we all started clapping our hands in the water?

Life's most precious resource is leaving us.

Once Gone -
It's Gone Forever
by Don Ford

Water cascades over the brink
Falling, spilling endlessly
No effort expended in the fall
Always leaving, not returning

Gone but followed on its heels
Behind itself more water comes
Continues on in moving cycles
Tumbling, rumbling sounds heard

Rising bubbles and foam churning
At the bottom briskly carried off
Can water run and last forever?
Will it always quench the thirst?

How we care for these cool waters
Well determines what's in store
Someday, soon, brooks are silent
Maybe no more streams and rivers

Gone the sound of water lapping
Will shorelines matter any more?
Can we shake the guilt and blame?
The waters can never return again.

Author Notes

This is a free verse poem that is not meant to rhyme. Only time will tell how long before we use up this life giving flow. There are efforts under way to conserve this resource and to clean up the pollutants found in it.

But is there enough time left? We better all hope and pray there is! It seems that time is never on our side.

SPECIAL Note: This arrived this morning. A lake near us is being reclaimed and is starting to look pretty good. This is great news, since this lake has been on the worst water environmental list for some time.

One of many true stories I share about family life.

Stories in my Library

Gone Fishin' by Don Ford

To my sweet daughter and fishing buddy.

Author Notes:
I am a storyteller from the word go. Some of it is real and some of it is imagined. My goal is to entertain, maybe turn a few smiles right side up. An artist from my youth, I write and paint in different colors. Cheers.

Now don't everyone get all touchy fee-lie on me, and I will share what happened just this morning.

"Dad, are we going fishing today?" My daughter had been anticipating this for some time.

She began by relating to me that she could not sleep the night before. She woke up at 5 am, 6 am, 6:30 am, and here we were talking at 7 am.

"Yes, honey. I promised you if it weren't raining that we would hit the water."

"Do you want me to get ready right now?" She was more than excited.

"Sure babe, go ahead. Don't wear your good shoes." For the last three years, I had taken my girl fishing. Now at 11, she still wants to go, but never cares to put the worm on the hook.

When we arrived at Green Lakes State Park, the questions began. "Are we too early for the fish?" This question followed on the heels of, "Why do they take so long to bite?"

"We are here to learn first how to fish, and to also learn to be patient. So start with talking to me in a whisper, since they can hear us. Unless they are starving, they will eat when they feel like it."

"Dad, does the worm feel it when it goes on the hook? Does it hurt them?"

"You notice how careful I am, and I don't do it too fast. Maybe if I were too quick and rough it might hurt." I was hoping the questions wouldn't get any harder to answer.

"Dad, that butterfly keeps circling you over and over. Do you know what that means?"

"No, honey, but I bet you are going to tell me, aren't you?."

"That's right, I am. It means you are a gentle person. That's what my teacher told us in science class."

Later, I noticed the butterfly let me pick it up with my fingers. Shortly after this, a dragonfly landed on my shoulder, and my daughter said, "Hey, he likes you too, Dad."

But she remembers my famous dragonfly story that I sold to a magazine, where a lone dragonfly saved me from hoards of black-flies.

During today's little adventure we both caught a fish. This year was different; this year my fish and her fish were the same size. Other years she always caught the biggest fish. That of course remains our little secret, now doesn't it.

Today we only fished for a little over an hour and then headed home. By the time we got back, Mom was waiting to hear the tall tales.

"Mom, guess what? Dad exaggerated today. He said the fish we saw in the water was as big as a house."

"Show me how big it was." Then my daughter proceeded to stretch her hands as far apart as she could. "Wow, it sounds like your dad wasn't too far off."

Author Notes
There are moments in our lives that we hold on to dearly, this will always be one of those times, along with countless others.

Profile Information

DON G. FORD ; AKA dgford, grassroots08, greywolf

Favorite Quote: "the best writing is rewriting" - E.B. White

Sometimes he is up typing or writing into the wee hours, until his fingers fall off. Now you know he writes fiction, but he also writes in every other genre. Poetry is a specialty of his and he likes to experiment.

Storytelling is his keynote and he's paid very well. Shares at retirement homes, schools, and churches. He has a strong faith in his Creator and knows that we are all stewards of this worlds' environmental resources.

What Do You Write?

Poetry, Fiction, Non Fiction, Children's, Play-writing, Other

How Many Years Have You Been Writing?

It all began at age 15, so quite a while.

Favorite Books and Authors: **E. B. White (For the kid in me)**

Western authors too numerous to list (For the Cowboy in me) Robert Louis Stevenson, Frost and a host of others (For the Poet in me) Hitchcock and H.G. Wells (Figure this one out yourself)

Guess Who's Hiding at the Alphabet Zoo?

Don Ford

Life is all about variety, and no where is that truer than in the animal kingdom. There are different kinds of dogs, horses, fish, rabbits; you name it.

This book will take you into the lives of many of those animals. If you didn't care before, or know that you should, remember that many of these creatures are vanishing from off the Earth. **List Price: $10.99 (FULL COLOR) https:// www.createspace.com/430777**

The purpose of this compilation of short stories, vignettes, and poems is to turn a few smiles right side up. You'll run into spiders, ghosts and even the little "Fly on the Wall". It's all in fun and for everyone's reading pleasure. If you have your boots on, jump right in. Every chapter here is a...

Publication Date: March 28, 2013

List Price: $7.99

https://www.createspace.com/

4203459

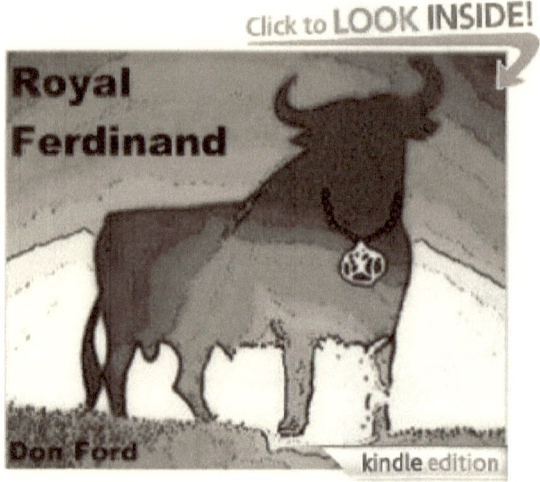

$0.99 Nook Book Reading

Royal Ferdinand [NOOK Book]Attention parents and Grandparents. Great read!

Overview Friends come in all sizes, colors, and species. Children and those young at heart will enjoy this display of simple fun as we look into the lives of two very different characters, who we find in the end are not so different. This tale is really for the kid in all of us. A fun loving, carefree, and learning experience for children today.